4.49
D
.W ②

DRAMA CL

The Drama Class............ .... world's
greatest plays in aⁿᵒⁱᵘᵃᵇⁱᵉ paperback editions for students,
actors and theatregoers. The hallmarks of the series are
accessible introductions, uncluttered texts and an overall
theatrical perspective.

Given that readers may be encountering a particular play
for the first time, the introduction seeks to fill in the
theatrical/historical background and to outline the chief
themes rather than concentrate on interpretational and
textual analysis. Similarly the play-texts themselves are free
of footnotes and other interpolations: instead there is an
end-glossary of 'difficult' words and phrases.

The texts of the English-language plays in the series
have been prepared taking full account of all existing
scholarship. The foreign-language plays have been newly
translated into a modern English that is both actable and
accurate: many of the translators regularly have their work
staged professionally.

Edited until his early death by Kenneth McLeish, the
Drama Classics series continues with his aim of providing
a first-class library of dramatic literature representing the
best of world theatre.

Associate editors:
Professor Trevor R. Griffiths
Dr. Colin Counsell
School of Arts and Humanities
Universit y of North London

DRAMA CLASSICS *the first hundred*

The Alchemist
All for Love
Andromache
Antigone
Arden of Faversham
Bacchae
Bartholomew Fair
The Beaux Stratagem
The Beggar's Opera
Birds
Celestina
The Changeling
A Chaste Maid in
   Cheapside
The Cherry Orchard
Children of the Sun
El Cid
The Country Wife
Cyrano de Bergerac
The Dance of Death
The Devil is an Ass
Doctor Faustus
A Doll's House
Don Juan
The Duchess of Malfi
Edward II
Electra (Euripides)
Electra (Sophocles)
An Enemy of the
   People
Every Man in his
   Humour
Everyman
Faust
A Flea in her Ear
Frogs
Fuenteovejuna
The Game of Love
   and Chance
Ghosts
The Government
   Inspector

Hedda Gabler
The Hypochondriac
The Importance of
   Being Earnest
An Ideal Husband
An Italian Straw Hat
The Jew of Malta
The Knight of the
   Burning Pestle
The Lady from the Sea
The Learned Ladies
Lady Windermere's
   Fan
Life is a Dream
The Lower Depths
The Lucky Chance
Lulu
Lysistrata
The Magistrate
The Malcontent
The Man of Mode
The Marriage of
   Figaro
Mary Stuart
The Master Builder
Medea
The Misanthrope
The Miser
Miss Julie
A Month in the
   Country
A New Way to Pay
   Old Debts
Oedipus
The Oresteia
Peer Gynt
Phedra
The Playboy of the
   Western World
The Recruiting Officer
The Revenger's
   Tragedy

The Rivals
The Roaring Girl
La Ronde
Rosmersholm
The Rover
The School for
   Scandal
The Seagull
The Servant of Two
   Masters
She Stoops to
   Conquer
The Shoemakers'
   Holiday
Six Characters in
   Search of an
   Author
The Spanish Tragedy
Spring's Awakening
Summerfolk
Tartuffe
Thérèse Raquin
Three Sisters
'Tis Pity She's a
   Whore
Too Clever by Half
Ubu
Uncle Vanya
Volpone
The Way of the
   World
The White Devil
The Wild Duck
A Woman of No
   Importance
Women Beware
   Women
Women of Troy
Woyzeck

*The publishers welcome
suggestions for further titles*

DRAMA CLASSICS

ANTIGONE

by
Sophocles

translated and with an introduction by
Marianne McDonald

NICK HERN BOOKS
London
www.nickhernbooks.co.uk

A Drama Classic

This edition of *Antigone* first published in Great Britain
as a paperback original in 2000 by Nick Hern Books Limited,
14 Larden Road, London W3 7ST

Reprinted 2004

Typeset by Country Setting, Kingsdown, Kent CT14 8ES
Printed and bound in Great Britain by Bookmarque, Croydon,
Surrey

A CIP catalogue record for this book is available from
the British Library

ISBN 1 85459 200 9

Introduction

Sophocles

Sophocles was born at Colonus near Athens in about 496
BC and died in 406 BC. He was spared the sight of
Athens' final defeat at the hands of Sparta in 404 BC.

Sophocles was a model citizen. He acted as *Hellenotamias*
('a treasurer,' 443/2) in the league Athens organized after
the Peace of Callias with Persia. He studied dance and
was said to have danced around the trophy after the
battle of Salamis. He also served as a general dealing with
the Samian revolt in 441. Some say that the *Antigone*
earned him this position. Others suggest that Sophocles'
disgust at the exposure of the enemies' corpses might have
led him to write this play. After the Sicilian defeat in 413
BC he was one of the *Probouloi* ('special Athenian officials')
elected to deal with the political aftermath of the disaster.

Sophocles followed in Aeschylus' footsteps by serving his
city when he could, in either a political or a cultural
function. He lived to about 90, and it is said that he was
sued by one of his sons, who claimed he was no longer
capable of managing his own affairs. His defence was to
read lines from the recently written *Oedipus at Colonus*, and
he was acquitted. The story of a lawsuit is probably
spurious, since there is other testimony that Sophocles got

on well with both of his sons. Phrynichus (the comic poet) wrote that 'Sophocles lived to a ripe old age, and he was happy and clever. After writing many excellent tragedies, he died well without suffering any serious misfortune.' Perhaps a fragment from one of Sophocles' plays may reveal his own outlook: 'It is fairest to live justly, and most profitable to live healthily, but the sweetest is to have a bit of love each day'.

The ancients regarded Sophocles as a man at ease with himself and contented with life. In Plato's *Republic* Sophocles is reported to have claimed that he was happy that he was finally free from that wild taskmaster, love. After his death he was said to have become a sacred hero like Oedipus, and was worshipped as Dexion, roughly translatable as 'he who receives'. because of his association with the cult of Asclepius, which he had helped to introduce into Athens after the plague. He also was a priest of the healing spirit Halon.

Sophocles is the playwright of heroism. His Antigone is the first female character in drama to be a hero in the full sense of the word. She is the first conscientious objector. The play is often performed as veiled criticism of an abusive government to show that something is rotten in that particular state.

Even at his or her best, it is difficult to feel empathy towards a Sophoclean hero, who is both alienated and alienating, but one has to admire the single-minded pursuit of goals that so often entail self-destruction, along with the destruction of others. As Bernard Knox says, 'Sophocles creates a tragic universe in which man's heroic

action, free and responsible, brings him sometimes
through suffering to victory but more often to a fall which
is both defeat and victory at once; the suffering and glory
are fused in an indissoluble unity'.

Sophocles shows his characters struggling to right the
wrongs they perceive in the world about them, and there
is some objective justification for their struggles. What
Sophoclean heroes do, they also do in isolation. Antigone
goes to her death alone, as does Ajax. They die for
ideals, which, although somewhat misguided in their
one-sidedness, can still be respected. Sophocles celebrates
the hero, whereas Euripides (as we shall see later) laments
the victim. Sophocles is a master of character and of the
language that creates character. He steers a path between
the grandeur of Aeschylus and the witty colloquialisms
of Euripides.

Antigone: **What Happens in the Play**

In Sophocles' Theban plays, Laius, king of Thebes, was
given a prophecy that he would be killed by his son.
So when his son Oedipus was born, Laius ordered that
he should be left on a mountainside to die. The servant
commanded to abandon the baby took pity on him, and
gave him to a shepherd who brought him to the king of
Corinth to be raised by the royal family. The Delphic
oracle told Oedipus he would kill his father and marry
his mother. He left Corinth to escape this fate, but killed
a man at a crossroads, who, unknown to him, was his
father. He arrived in Thebes. After saving the people
from the sphinx who was ravaging the land, he married

the queen, his mother, Jocasta. He had two sons by her, Eteocles and Polyneices, and two daughters, Antigone and Ismene. A plague struck and he was identified as the source of the pollution. Jocasta committed suicide. Having cursed his sons, Oedipus went to Colonus to die. The sons agreed to alternate the rule of Thebes, but Eteocles refused to give up the throne. Polyneices attacked Thebes with the help of forces from Argos. They killed each other in the fight. Creon, brother of Jocasta, has now taken over the rule of Thebes and issued a proclamation forbidding burial of Polyneices.

The play opens after a war between Eteocles, the city's ruler, and Polyneices, his brother, who has attacked the city. Both died in the encounter. Their uncle Creon, the new ruler, decrees that Eteocles should be buried, but not Polyneices. Against the warnings of her sister Ismene, Antigone tries to bury her brother's body. For this act of defiance, Creon condemns Antigone to be confined in what will become a tomb, with just enough food and water so that the city will avoid the pollution of her death. His son Haemon, who is engaged to be married to her, protests and says that the people of Thebes are on his side, but they are too afraid of Creon to speak up. The prophet Teiresias tells Creon he must bury the body of Polyneices. He reluctantly gives in. He finds Antigone has hanged herself. Haemon attacks him in the rocky tomb, then falls on his own sword, embracing Antigone as he dies. Eurydice, Haemon's mother, hears of his death and stabs herself. Creon is a broken man at the end. Both he and Antigone have paid a high price for their refusal to compromise. The chorus conclude with apt words:

If a person is to be happy he needs good sense.
Never show disrespect to the gods.
Loud words from those with high pretensions
Lead to heavy blows of punishment;
Good sense is hammered out on the anvil of age.

Antigone

Antigone is the first, and remains the greatest, play in western literature about the consequences of individual conscience defying civil authority. In her clash with King Creon, as she defends the rights of the family, Antigone invokes 'the unwritten law of the gods', whereas Creon rests his case on defending the safety and security of the state against anarchy. Both he and Antigone break their heads on the principle the other represents, one the law of the city, and the other the family. In this play Sophocles is suggesting that a humane city's laws should be based on recognition of the rights of the family, and respect for the gods.

These protagonists do not give up. Both Creon and Antigone suffer from their inability to compromise. This play is a human drama and a tragedy that shows two passionate people who, in their determination to defend their positions, end up destroying themselves and others. The price of supporting their beliefs is paid in human blood.

Antigone's hot-headedness is particularly clear in a couple of brutal exchanges with her sister. Nevertheless she is indisputably a heroine who knows her duty to her family. Here her duty lies: to her beloved brother and the unwritten laws of the gods.

Creon opposes Antigone with the might of law, on which he says personal happiness is based, namely via a well-controlled city. What Antigone does is the opposite of what Socrates recommends: he declared that he would follow the city's laws even if the decision was unjust (*Crito*). With Sophocles' usual dramatic economy, Antigone is punished by the ruler and the *polis* (the city) she opposes, and Creon is punished by the loss of his own family, whose values he subordinated to those of the *polis*.

Justification can be found for Creon's refusing burial to an enemy, though this view is unpopular in some circles. It was clearly acceptable law to refuse burial to traitors in the city. Just as heroes were celebrated, enemies and particularly traitors were punished. Polyneices chose to wage war against his native city, and even if his brother refused to share the rule of Thebes, as it had been arranged after the death of Oedipus, this was not sufficient justification to bring an army against one's own people.

Sophocles never presents us with black vs. white, heroes vs. villains. As Oscar Wilde said, 'A thing is not necessarily true because a man dies for it.' One may even claim that the play should be called the *Creon*, because it is more his tragedy. Sophocles' Ajax declares that a noble man ought either to live with honour, or die with honour (479–80). Creon did neither. He aimed at honour, but missed through the excessiveness of the pursuit. He loses a son and his wife dies cursing him. He has lost honour along with his family. He is right to say that he is less than nothing and a walking corpse.

Creon is well named, because his name means ruler
and he rules in an absolute way. He represents the law
of the city, defends it, and finally yields to the pressures
of the prophet Teiresias and the chorus. At first he is
unbending, as Haemon points out, but he is constantly
forced to modify his position, agreeing first not to include
Ismene in her sister's harsh punishment, then finally
allowing Polyneices' burial and Antigone's release – but
too late. His is the rigidity of the Sophoclean hero, the
tree that will not bend to save itself when the river is in
flood (ll. 712–14). The ruler who will not listen to his
people, or even his family, and claims he should be
obeyed whether right or wrong (ll. 666–67), may end
up losing both, as does Creon. He gains in knowledge,
accepts blame, and concludes that he is nothing, less
than nobody (ll. 1317–25). He does not have the grandeur
of Oedipus, but he shares his suffering. Contrary to
Oedipus he learns in spite of himself rather than because
of himself.

Antigone is equally unbending. Her curse on Creon is
fulfilled and he is made to suffer what she did and worse.

Creon, Oedipus and Antigone are impatient and easily
angered. They lash out at those closest to them (Oedipus's
impatient anger led him to kill his father). The chorus
calls Antigone a law unto herself, *autonomos* (l. 821), and
she resembles Creon and Oedipus in this also. One might
even argue that what she does is totally ineffectual, and, in
fact, leads to innocent deaths in addition to her own. It is
only Teiresias and his dire prophecy that brings about
Polyneices' burial.

Antigone kills herself rather than wait and suffer more humiliation. Creon is made to realise his mistakes by Teiresias, and goes to release Antigone, but her suicide prevents his freeing her. She is found first by Haemon, who has come to rescue her. Like Romeo, he arrives too late and decides to join his beloved in death. Haemon dies in what seems to be a perverted marriage ritual, a 'marriage to death'. Antigone speaks of her marriage to Hades, and it may in fact be her veil with which she hangs herself (a veil figured in the marriage ritual). Haemon's name is derived from the Greek word for blood, and when he takes his life, his blood spurts out over Antigone's cheek in a type of consummation.

This play, as others by Sophocles, is riddled with imagery. Disease, wild and tame animals, ships, and rigidity, are all recurrent images. Most of these images have to do with power and control. Creon says of Antigone: 'It's the stubborn spirit that's more prone to fall than others; it's the toughest iron that snaps and shatters' (ll. 473-76). Haemon accuses his father of being unbending, and says, 'In winter storms the trees that bend save themselves, but those that resist are destroyed root and branch. It's the same with a ship: when the wind is strong, if you sheet in the sails too much, the boat will capsize' (ll. 712 17). He illustrates his rigidity even when he follows Teiresias' advice; instead of releasing Antigone, she being alive and urgently in need of attention, he goes off to bury Polyneices, who could certainly have waited a little longer, being dead already. It is Creon's nature to attend to the man first, and to carry out what is beneficial for the city.

A theme that runs throughout the play is the opposition of male against female. Creon says that he will not be made a female nor be bested by one (e.g., ll. 484-85, 525). It turns out that he will weep at the end like a woman and that he is in fact bested by Antigone. He goes inside the house at the end, the woman's territory, whereas Antigone braved the man's world by burying her brother and being led out of the city.

Ismene acts as a foil to Antigone. This allows us to appreciate the difference between a compliant citizen and a conscientious objector. Antigone is harsh and cruel towards her sister. For someone who claims that she is by nature one who prefers friendship to enmity, she is extreme in her rejection of Ismene. Her motive might be to save Ismene's life by showing that she was not implicated. Perhaps Antigone also needs to reject Ismene's softness so strongly because she recognizes how much easier it would be to be like her. Antigone's heroic posture may need this negative buttress. Ismene, however, is willing to die at her sister's side. Antigone is like her father, Oedipus, who always went too far.

The guard is a wonderful contrast to Creon, who threatens torture and treats him like a slave. Their encounter illuminates Haemon's accusation to Creon: 'You're not ruling a desert, father, but a city with people' (l. 739). The guard is an everyday person, not at all interested in heroics, and thus (like Ismene) highlights Antigone's bold stand. Altruism and ideals vanish when it comes to saving his own skin. The messenger, too, shows that he is a reasonable and not very imaginative man. For instance, he is more concerned with decorum than pity for the queen when he comments that she knows her place and will mourn indoors rather than embarrass anyone by ordering a public lamentation (ll. 1246-50).

Haemon and Ismene represent what reasonable and sympathetic people will do. They have neither the fanaticism of the heroes, nor the mundane concerns of the guard and messenger. Haemon and Ismene both show their loyalty to those they love. Their positions are understandable and certainly at the beginning they are good citizens. Rather like Rosencrantz and Guildenstern, their fates are tied to the heroic monsters who direct the plot.

Choruses

A modern audience might expect the chorus to voice more opposition to Creon. But we remember that he holds absolute power over the chorus, and this can explain much of their deferential action. They also may in fact agree with him (we do not have to believe Haemon).

The first chorus celebrates a victory, and this communal joy contrasts with the individual suffering of Antigone. It is light coming before the dark. The second chorus is about what man can accomplish and what are his limitations (death, and impiety or evil acts which will be punished). This translation gives *deinos*, as 'amazing.' It can mean 'wonderful,' 'awesome,' 'great,' but also 'terrible,' and 'monstrous.' We get the modern word 'dinosaur' from it, 'monster lizard.' This word can apply to any Sophoclean hero: they are great in their capacity for both good and evil.

The third chorus talks of the evils that haunt a family for generations. This certainly applies to the family of Oedipus which has been living under a family curse since Laius. This chorus also preaches against excess. One recalls the Delphic maxim, 'Nothing in Excess.' A tragic hero will often do everything in excess.

The fourth chorus is about love. Love was often regarded as a disease in antiquity. A girl's cheeks are mentioned, and Haemon will die staining Antigone's cheek. Love leads to madness and violence, and indeed will lead Haemon to violence against himself, as it also leads Antigone to bury her brother. In her case love is joined to duty.

The fifth chorus talks of various mythical characters who were imprisoned or confined as Antigone was. This gives a type of elevation to her, by associating her with the figures of heroic legend.

Like the first chorus, the final chorus invokes Dionysus, the god of the theatre, and lord of the dance. The audience hopes for a happy ending, because Creon will finally follow Teiresias' advice. But Dionysus, whom Euripides characterized as both most fierce (*deinotatos*) and most gentle to man (*êpiôtatos*, *Bacchae* l. 861), will in this case be more fierce than gentle. Like man, as character-ized in the second chorus, Dionysus can be both awesome and awful.

The last choral comment, that good sense is hammered in by age, reworks Aeschylus' tragic message in the *Oresteia* that man must learn by suffering. In tragedy, learning often comes too late.

Original Staging

Antigone was probably performed in 443 or 441 BC in the fifth-century theatre of Dionysus in Athens which was outdoors, and featured a circular playing area called the orchestra. It may have had an altar in the centre. It was built into the side of the hill on whose summit was the Acropolis on which the Parthenon stands.

This theatre seated about 15,000 to 18,000 people, from a population of about 300,000 in Attica, comprised of male citizens, women, children, slaves and foreign residents. It is likely that only males attended the theatre.

The main Athenian dramatic festival was called the Greater Dionysia, in honour of the god of theatre, Dionysus. The Greater Dionysia was held in early spring, the 9th-13th days of the month Elaphebolion (March/April), when the seas were calm and Athenian allies could safely make the sea journey and attend. On the first day there was an elaborate show of tribute from the allies, war orphans were paraded, and prominent citizens were given awards. It was very much like the May Day parade in Russia, when Soviet power was at its height. Going to the theatre was a social, civic, and religious event. One purpose of the festival was to impress foreigners.

Three or four days of the Greater Dionysia were devoted to plays. The performances began at dawn and lasted all day. There are several plays whose action begins at dawn, or even in the dark.

Three playwrights were selected to put on their work at the Great Dionysia. Each provided a quartet of plays,

three tragedies and one satyr play that comically handled
tragic themes. A comedy by a different playwright
followed, or was shown on a different day. There are
three major tragic playwrights in fifth-century Athens
whose works we have: Aeschylus (525-456 BC), seven
of whose plays survive out of approximately eighty;
Sophocles (ca. 496-406 BC), with seven plays out of
approximately 123; and Euripides (ca. 480-406 BC), with
nineteen out of approximately ninety. Aristotle tells us
that Aeschylus added a second actor and that Sophocles
added a third, creating more possibilities for interchange
and conflict. Aeschylus preferred the connected trilogy
that allowed the development of a concept such as the
workings of divine justice over several generations. The
only connected trilogy that has survived is Aeschylus'
Oresteia. Sophocles abandoned the practice of writing
connected trilogies and instead preferred to highlight
a major character within three single plays. Euripides
probably did not write connected trilogies either, but
instead of emphasizing one heroic character, as Sophocles
did, he usually divided his emphasis and created a more
socially directed drama.

A prize was given for the best tragic poet and for the best
comic poet. The audience were part of the performance
and openly expressed their feelings and reactions, which
very likely influenced the judging. The *chorêgos* (person who
paid for the costuming and training of the chorus) was
also given a prize if his playwright won. The jury was
selected from the citizens.

Sophocles is said never to have been placed third when
he competed. He first competed in 468 BC, when he

defeated Aeschylus, and was awarded the prize 24 times
(18 at the Greater Dionysia) in contrast to Aeschylus' 13
and Euripides' 4 or 5.

All the actors were male and masked, playing both male
and female roles. Masks with their stylized features
allowed the characters to be better recognized by the
audience in the large outdoor playing spaces in which the
tragedies were originally performed. The three actors were
later called Protagonist, Deuteragonist, and Tritagonist
(first, second, and third actor), and the roles were divided
between them, the major roles being taken by the
Protagonist. There were also supernumeraries (extras),
or non-speaking parts, such as attendants and children.
At first all the actors were non-professional, and the
playwright acted too. It is said that Sophocles' weak
voice prevented him from acting in his own plays.
He probably remained as what we would now call the
director. Eventually acting became professional, and prizes
were then awarded to actors too.

The number of people in the chorus was either twelve (as
in most plays by Aeschylus) or fifteen (Sophocles). They
generally remained present throughout the performance
after their first entrance and danced in the *orchestra* as they
sang. The music was provided by the *aulos*, a reed
instrument (like the oboe), and sometimes drums. Spoken
portions of the drama, mainly in iambic trimeter (a
rhythm closest to that of ordinary speech), alternated with
the choruses, which were always in lyric meters and
usually arranged in strophes and antistrophes ('turns' and
'turnings back', possibly referring to their danced
accompaniment). Anapaests, arrangements of two short

syllables followed by one long one ($\smile \smile -$), create a strong marching rhythm in the texts that accompany the initial entrance and final exit of the chorus.

The spoken part of a play could consist of a monologue, or a dialogue between two or three characters or some exchange with a chorus. Sometimes the dialogue took the form of one-line interchanges. At other times an actor bursts out into an impassioned lyric aria. Sometimes there was a formal lament, usually sung by an actor with the chorus.

According to Aristotle, Sophocles introduced scene-painting to suggest a visual background. Dead bodies could be displayed on a device called the *ekkyklêma* which was rolled out from the centre doors of the building depicted on the *skênê* (backdrop, literally 'tent'). This device showed stationary tableaux inside the *skênê*. A *mêchanê* ('machine,' or mechanical crane) allowed aerial entrances and exits, usually of the gods. It is doubtful that Aeschylus used any of these devices before the *Oresteia* in 458; the other playwrights used them sparingly. They were very popular from the fourth century on. The use of side entrances and exits, *parodoi*, could indicate whether a character was local or from a foreign region, or going to or coming from a particular place.

Performance History

The more popular plays were often revived in the fourth century. During these revivals they were vulnerable to adaptation and additions by actors and producers. Around 330 BC, the Athenian politician Lycurgus prescribed that copies of the texts of the plays should be deposited in official archives, and that future performances should conform to these texts. These copies were lent to the Egyptian king, Ptolemy Euergetes I, and passed into the library at Alexandria, to form the basis of the critical edition made by the Librarian, Aristophanes of Byzantium (ca. 257-180 BC). Although the performance tradition is not well documented for this period, the plays continued to be widely read, and scholars in Alexandria wrote commentaries on them, parts of which still survive. But by the second to third century AD, the number of plays that were being read had diminished. The seven plays of Aeschylus and the seven of Sophocles which survive were the only ones which were still available for performance. Of Euripides there were ten such plays, but a further nine of his survive through a lucky accident, preserved in a manuscript which presents them in a quasi-alphabetical order (they evidently formed one part of a collection representing The Complete Euripides).

After the Athenian Academy was closed in 529 AD, classical texts and performance disappeared from sight for several centuries and did not reemerge until the revival of learning in the early Byzantine period.

Printed texts of all three playwrights were available from the early sixteenth century in Europe.

Plays are often used in repressive conditions to reveal the truth when mass media like newspapers, radio or television have been silenced by censorship. Sophocles' *Antigone* is often performed whenever a country is in trouble. This play resonates with timeless immediacy in situations of conflict.

Anouilh wrote an *Antigone* for occupied Paris in 1944, in which Antigone is the archetype of the oppressed. In Brecht's 1948 *Die Antigone des Sophokles*, based on Hölderlin's translation, Brecht gave Creon fascist overtones. In Tom Paulin's *The Riot Act*, set in the North of Ireland, his Antigone is a freedom fighter like Bernadette Devlin, and his Creon's words immediately bring to mind Ian Paisley. Brendan Kennelly also sees the Irish relevance in his *Antigone*, with its deadly net of words strangling substantive action. Aidan Carl Mathews has a tragic comedy called *Antigone*, which shares a lot with Beckett: bitter laughter echoing down the draughty corridors of history. All these works were performed or written in 1984, the same year that Athol Fugard's *The Island* appeared at Dublin's Gate theatre. In this play, written in South Africa in the early seventies and first performed in London in 1975, two prisoners perform *Antigone* in prison to keep their sanity in the midst of the insanity of Apartheid. In 1988, Andrzej Wajda had his chorus dressed with miners' helmets cheer Antigone at an international festival of ancient Greek drama at Delphi.

The translation of the play in this volume conveys all the essential ideas of the original. It is meant to be actable, so sound is important. The language is kept simple, a bit elevated in the choruses, but sometimes quite informal. The guard contrasts in this way with other characters, rather like the porter in *Macbeth*.

The first performance of this translation was in Cork, Ireland (1999), directed by Athol Fugard, with an international cast. In July, 2000 a new production was performed at the international theatre festival celebrating the millennium at Delphi by the DonAd company, an Irish troupe under the direction of Donal Courtney. Both Patricia Logue and Maeve McGrath, the actresses that played Antigone in the two productions, came from Belfast. In the DonAd version, the Gaelic singing by Colm Suilleabhin besides the use of *bodhrans* (Irish drums) to recall the banging of dustbins in the North of Ireland (a way to indicate the approach of the enemy), restore to this Greek tragedy not only its music but also its political atmosphere. The haunting Irish pipe replicated the ancient *aulos*. Music and singing were important elements of Greek tragedy, and modern performances benefit from their inclusion.

As Luke Clancy said in a review of the Fugard production: 'the *Antigone* has a habit of turning up when the political chips are down, with this particular version directed towards peace process Ireland. There may be, Sophocles and McDonald whisper to anyone who will listen, a tremendous moral power in compromise' (*The Times*, July 21, 1999). Flor Dullea said of the latest Irish performance by DonAd in Cork, 'The tragedy of Antigone came across to us with its dignity intact and we mourned the arrogance of those in power who use their positions to wreak vengeance on whom-so-ever dares to

show independence of spirit. History does repeat itself'
(Ireland's *Southern Star*, May 13, 2000).

Antigone and Creon speak to all people at all times who
are concerned about and struggle over what is honourable.

Marianne McDonald

Further Reading

B. M. W. Knox, *The Heroic Temper: Studies in Sophoclean Tragedy*. Berkeley (1964) is a good introduction to the character of the Sophoclean hero. Charles Segal, *Tragedy and Civilization: An Interpretation of Sophocles* (1981) and *Sophocles' Tragic World: Divinity, Nature, Society* (1995) give useful commentary. George Steiner, *Antigones: How the Antigone Legend has Endured in Western Literature, Art and Thought* (1984) traces its historical evolution. J. Michael Walton, *The Greek Sense of Theatre*, 2nd ed. (1996) and *Living Greek Theatre: A Handbook of Classical Performance and Modern Production* (1987) are very helpful in giving background for the Greek theatre, interpretation, and also more performance history.

Sophocles: Key Dates

NB All dates are BC

c. 496   Sophocles born.

468   First competed against Aeschylus.

443-2   Treasurer of Athena.

443
or 441   *Antigone.*

c. 442   *Ajax.*

441   General with Pericles (Samian Revolt).

431-404 Peloponnesian War.

c. 432   *Women of Trachis.*

c. 427   *Oedipus Tyrannus.*

c. 413   *Electra.* One of the *symbouloi* after Sicilian defeat.

409   *Philoctetes.*

406   Died.

401   *Oedipus at Colonus* performed posthumously.

ANTIGONE

Characters

ANTIGONE (Ant-TI as in it-go-knee)
ISMENE (Is-MEE-nee)
CREON (KREE-on)
HAEMON (HIGH-mon)
TEIRESIAS (Tie-REE-see-ass)
GUARD
MESSENGER
EURYDICE (You-RID-ih-see)
CHORUS

It is night.

ANTIGONE

Sweet Ismene, my dearest sister, you know how much we've suffered; how we have had to live with the sins of our father Oedipus, and all that they brought – pain, shame, and humiliation. And now, after all that, this new proclamation from our ruler. Have you heard about it? Or don't you care about what our enemies are doing to us?

ISMENE

I've heard nothing since our two brothers killed each other; nothing either good or bad since the invading army left.

ANTIGONE

That is why I've called you outside away from the others. I wanted to speak to you alone and tell you what I've heard.

ISMENE

What is it? You frighten me, Antigone.

ANTIGONE

Yes. I want to frighten you. Creon has honoured one of our brothers with burial and dishonoured the other. He has buried Eteocles in proper observance of right and custom, so that he can be honoured among the dead below. But he has forbidden anyone to bury or weep for Polyneices. His body must be left unmourned, without a tomb, a feast for scavenging birds. This is the worthy Creon's decree; he's coming here in person to spell it out. He doesn't take this lightly: anyone defying the proclamation is to be stoned to death. Yes. That's the situation. So now you have the chance to show whether you are true to your noble birth, or a coward.

ISMENE

My poor sweet Antigone. But, if this is so, what can we do about it?

ANTIGONE

I have a plan. Are you prepared to join me?

ISMENE

You frighten me again. What do you want us to do?

ANTIGONE

Will you help me honour the dead?

ISMENE

Bury Polyneices? But you've just said that's forbidden.

ANTIGONE

I shall bury our brother, even if you don't want to. I, for one, will not betray him.

ISMENE

You are out of your mind Antigone. Creon is the law.

ANTIGONE

He has no right to come between my brother and me.

ISMENE

Sister, remember how our father blinded himself when he discovered that he had killed his father and slept with his own mother. He died, hated and condemned by all! Then his wife and mother (one and the same), and she was our mother as well, brought her life to a violent end by hanging herself. And now, finally, our two poor brothers, on a single day, kill each other. And are we going to add to that cycle of horrors? We shall die if we go against the decision of the ruler. We are helpless women, Antigone, not made to fight against men. We are ruled by the more powerful; we must obey this order and if necessary even worse. I shall obey those who stand in authority, but I shall beg those under the earth to understand I'm being forced to do this against my will. It's mad to fight a battle you can't win.

ANTIGONE

Fine. I wouldn't let you help me now even if you wanted to; I don't want you at my side after what you've just said. Do as you like; I shall bury my brother. I know it's right, die if I must! My crime will be a holy crime. I am his and I shall lie buried with him. There will be more time with those below than those on earth. I'll be there for eternity. But as for you, forget about the gods, if that's what you want.

ISMENE

That's not what I want. I just can't break the laws of the city.

ANTIGONE

Make that excuse if you like. I'm going to bury our brother.

ISMENE

Oh, poor sister, I'm so afraid for you!

ANTIGONE

Don't worry about me; just take care of yourself.

ISMENE

At least keep your plan secret, and I'll do the same.

ANTIGONE

No! Go and tell everyone! I'll despise you all the more if you try to keep it secret. Let the whole world know what Antigone is going to do.

ISMENE

Creon will soon cool that hot heart of yours!

ANTIGONE

The ones that count will thank me well enough.

ISMENE

If you succeed, but you won't.

ANTIGONE

Only death will stop me; your words can't.

ISMENE

You're in love with the impossible. And I'm afraid.

ANTIGONE

If that's all you have to say, then you are my enemy, and Polyneices will have every right to call you that as well. So let me suffer for what you call impossible, because

I know that whatever I suffer, I, at least, shall die with
honour.

ISMENE

Then go, Antigone. There's nothing I can do to stop you.
But know that I'll always love you.

ANTIGONE *and* ISMENE *exeunt.*
The CHORUS *enters the orchestra.*
The sun rises and the stage is bathed in light.

CHORUS

First ray of sun, fairer than any seen before
By Thebes of the seven gates,
At last you appear,
Golden eye of day
Glancing over the streams of Dirce;
You made the man who came from Argos flee,
When, decked out in white armour and trappings,
He attacked our land.
This war was brought upon us
By that man of many quarrels, Polyneices.
He flew against us with piercing scream,
Like an eagle on wings as white as snow;
He came with many weapons
And helmets tossing their horse-hair plumes high;`
He stood above our houses,
Ringing them with spears hungry for gore,
But he fled before they had tasted our blood,
Before the fire of Hephaestus' pine torches
Had seized the crown of our towers.
Such was the din of war beating his back;
He was no match for the dragon race of Thebes.

Zeus hates a boastful tongue.
Seeing them advance in full force
With the overweening pride of shimmering gold,
Just as one reaches the highest towers
And prepares to bellow victory,
Zeus brings him down with his lightning bolt.

Down he falls and hits the hard earth,
That fire-bearer who raged, a wild Bacchant in his mad
    attack,
And breathed on us the blasts of hostile winds.
His plan to take the city went awry.
The worthy war-god gave victory to one, defeat to another;
Shattering the enemy he raced our chariot to victory.
Seven spearmen for seven gates,
Matched equal to equal;
Six won and gave their all-bronze weapons
To Zeus the trophy-collector,
While six fell defeated.
But at the seventh gate the ill-fated brothers,
Born of one father and one mother,
Clashed their spears, and
Both lost, sharing a double death.

Since glorious Victory has come
Answering with joy the joy of Thebes,
Let us forget the war
And dance our victory into the night.
We shall visit the shrines of the gods;
May Bacchus be the lord of a dance
That will shake the land of Thebes.

But here is our leader

Newly appointed by the fortune of war.
Why does he ask for this talk with his elder citizens?

Enter CREON.

CREON

Gentlemen, the gods shook our city with a heavy storm,
but now they have set things right again. I have singled
you out from all the rest because I know how loyal you
were to Laius' government and afterwards, when Oedipus
ran the city, you were loyal to him, and when he died
your loyalty carried through to his sons. Now that they
are dead, I hold all the power since I am their closest
relative.

You cannot know a man's heart, thought and judgement until you have tested his skill in leadership and
lawmaking. Any ruler who does not pursue the policies
he judges best, but holds his tongue because he is afraid,
I think him the lowest of the low. Worse still, a man
who sets a friend or relative above his country doesn't
deserve the name of citizen. Speaking for myself, I
wouldn't keep quiet if I saw the city threatened with
destruction. And I wouldn't call an enemy of my land a
friend of mine. I know our salvation is the ship of state
and only those who keep her on the right course can
be called her friends and benefactors. I plan to make
this city great.

And now I have an announcement for the people about
Oedipus' sons. Eteocles who died defending the city, a
great warrior and patriot, shall be buried in a tomb with
all the honours appropriate for the most heroic of our
dead. But, his brother Polyneices, a fugitive from his

native land, and his gods, and his relatives, who came to
burn this city to the ground, drink our blood, and lead us
into slavery, I decree that he shall have no funeral and no
mourning. His corpse will be left unburied, to be torn
apart and eaten by dogs and birds. Such is my decision.
Traitors will never be preferred over law-abiding citizens.
I will always honour the loyal subject whether he is alive
or dead.

CHORUS

It is your prerogative to punish disloyalty and to reward
loyalty. We know only too well the power you hold over
us, whether dead or alive.

CREON

So see that what I have decreed is done.

CHORUS

Can't you get someone younger to do it?

CREON

I'm not asking you to stand guard over the body. I have
men ready to do that.

CHORUS

Then, what else do you want from us?

CREON

No sympathy for lawbreakers.

CHORUS

No one's going to risk his life defying you.

CREON

You're right, death is the penalty if they do. But money
corrupts.

Enter GUARD.

GUARD

Your lordship, I don't say I'm exactly out of breath
coming here: my feet were a wee bit heavy. I kept
thinking and thinking, and this held me up; I went in
circles, determined to go back. My mind just wouldn't
stop talking, 'You bloody good for nothing, you're going
to be punished for what you have to say. So now, you
idiot, you're stopping? If Creon hears about what
happened from somebody else, how do you think you're
going to get out of trouble then?' Turning this over and
over, looking at it again and again, I dragged my feet,
and made a short road long. Finally I screwed up my
courage and decided to come. And here I am! Even if
what I say amounts to nothing, I'll still tell you the whole
story. I keep saying to myself I'll only suffer what is bound
to happen anyway.

CREON

What are you going on about, man?

GUARD

I want to tell you first I didn't do it, and I didn't see who
did, so you can't blame me.

CREON

Get on with it! It's clear you have something serious to
tell me.

GUARD

A weighty matter slows a man down!

CREON

For God's sake out with it – then you are free to go!

GUARD

OK, OK. I'll tell you. Someone has buried Polyneices and got away with it. Whoever it was scattered earth over the body, and performed burial rites.

CREON

What? Who would have dared?

GUARD

There was no sign that a pickaxe was used and the earth hadn't been turned over by a hoe; the ground was hard and dry, unbroken, no wheel marks either. Whoever did it left no trace. When the guard of the morning watch showed us it, we were desperate! We couldn't see the body: it wasn't exactly buried but there was a thin blanket of earth over it, just enough to satisfy the gods. There was no sign of bites from wild animals, or dogs. We badmouthed each other, one guard blaming the other, and we might have cracked a couple of skulls because there was nobody there to stop us. Any one of us could have done it, but you couldn't point the finger at a soul because nobody had seen anything. We were ready to go through fire, bog, and muck and swear by our mothers' lives we didn't do it, and we didn't know who'd planned or done it. To cut a long story short, when our search got us nowhere, somebody said something that made all our knees knock with fear, and we couldn't see any way out of this hellhole. He said we had to tell you and not hide a single thing. So that's what happened, and I was the poor bastard who got the short straw: I won the privilege of bringing you the good news. So here I am: unwilling and unwanted...don't think I don't know: nobody loves the messenger who brings bad news.

CHORUS

Could the gods be behind this?

CREON

That's ridiculous. Now you are making me angry. It is blasphemy to suggest that the gods have any interest in this corpse. Did they want him buried so they could load him with honours as a benefactor? He came to burn and loot their sacred temples and treasures, and destroy their land and its laws. Do you see the gods honouring traitors? Impossible! For a long time now people in the city who find me difficult have been muttering privately against me, reluctant to keep their necks under the yoke, as they should if they felt any loyalty to me. I see what's happened – they've bribed someone to do this. There is nothing worse than greed: it destroys cities; drives men out of their homes; perverts honourable minds and leads to crime. It teaches villainy and neglect of the gods. Those who were paid to do this will soon regret it! Listen closely: I swear that if you do not find the person responsible for the burial and bring him here to me, eternal hell shall be too short for you! I will hang you alive until you scream out your treachery and learn that I am your paymaster, and no one else. The bribes in your pocket won't protect you.

GUARD

Will your lordship allow me to put in a word, or am I to clear off just like that?

CREON

You're playing with fire.

GUARD

Is the fire in your ears or in your heart?

CREON

You want a map? What does it matter where the fire is?

GUARD

The one who did it burns your heart; I just burn your ears.

CREON

Stop rambling!

GUARD

Rambler, yes; criminal, no.

CREON

Yes! Because you sold your soul for money!

GUARD

It's a pity if a man can't tell false coin from true.

CREON

Stop being clever. If you do not bring me the guilty parties you'll pay with your blood for selling yourself.

Exit CREON.

GUARD

You can believe I want the person who did it found, but whether he will be or not, who knows? One thing for sure, you'll never see me here again. Now, thank God, I'm let off – who would have thought it possible?

Exit GUARD.

CHORUS

There are many wonders in the world,
But nothing more amazing than man!
He crosses the white-capped sea in winter's storms,
Cuts through the surge as it booms about him;
He harasses the almighty immortal unwearying Earth,
Turning his plough back and forth year after year,
Turning up the soil with the help of mules.

Skilful man of clever thought
Traps in the woven coils of his nets
The birds, with thoughts as light as wings,
And tribes of wild animals,
And sea creatures of the deep.
With his devices he overpowers
The wild beast that roams the mountain;
He tames the rough-maned horse
And the untiring mountain bull,
Hurling a yoke over their necks.

He has mastered speech
And thought as swift as the wind,
And the ways of government.
All-resourceful man
Knows how to flee the
Airborne arrows of ice and rain.
He is ready for all that comes,
As he goes out to meet the future;
He can cure terrible diseases;
Only death he cannot escape.

His contrivance is skilful beyond hope;
He moves sometimes towards good,

Sometimes towards evil.
When he follows the laws of the land
And swears to keep the justice of the gods,
He is lofty in the city; but exiled, and homeless
Is the man who consorts with evil
For the sake of greed and ambition.
He has my curse upon him;
He'll never be welcome in my house,
Nor a companion for my thoughts.

The chorus see ANTIGONE *who is brought in by* GUARD.

Am I imagining this? Can I believe my eyes?
Surely this is the young Antigone,
Unhappy daughter of an unhappy father.
Has she been caught disobeying the ruler's decree?

GUARD
Where is Creon? Creon? Creon?

CHORUS
Here he comes!

Enter CREON.

CREON
What is it? You again!

GUARD
She did it! We caught her burying the body. Sir, you can't count on anything! Second thoughts turn the first into a lie: I swore I'd never come here again because your threats scared the hell out of me! But the joy a person prays for and never thought he'd get is by far the best; so here I am, though I never fancied I would be – I caught

this wee girl burying the body. We didn't draw straws this time: the lucky mission was mine! Now sir, take her, judge her, convict her; but I'm free and it's my right to be out of this mess!

CREON

How did you catch her?

GUARD

She was burying the body with her own hands: that's the whole of it!

CREON

Do you realize what you're saying? Are you sure you've got it right?

GUARD

I saw her burying the body you said should be left unburied. Is that not clear enough for you?

CREON

Yes, but how did you come to see and catch her in the act?

GUARD

Well, this is how it was. When we got back after you threatened our lives, we swept off all the earth that covered the body, and made sure the decaying corpse was naked. Then we put the hill between us and the stink of the corpse, and we sat down. We kept each other awake with threats if we thought anybody was slacking off and not doing what he was supposed to do, keep watch that is. We kept this up until the roasting sun was directly above us and the heat was like an oven...the hour of the devils! Then suddenly a swirling wind raised a dust storm that filled the sky and covered the plain, and whipped the leaves on the trees. The dust was everywhere, so we shut our eyes to protect ourselves from this god-sent plague. And then when it finally let up, this wee girl comes into view. She screams a bitter heart-piercing cry like a mother bird who finds her nest empty, and her newborn young nowhere to be found. Just like that. When she sees the naked corpse, she screams, weeps, and groans, and calls down bitter curses on them that done it. Quickly she scatters earth over the corpse. Then she lifts up a bronze jug and pours a sacred offering of milk, honey and water over him. As soon as we saw this, we ran and hunted her down; when we charged her with this crime and the one before, she wasn't afraid. She didn't deny a thing; I was all mixed up – pleased and sad at the same time. I mean it's a pleasure to get out of trouble, but it is sad to make a wee girl suffer. But you know what they say: charity begins at home! And I'm let off!

CREON

You there, with your eyes on the ground. Do you admit or deny this?

ANTIGONE

I admit it; I deny nothing.

CREON (to GUARD)

You can be off, go where you please, you have escaped a heavy penalty.

Exit GUARD.

Now then Antigone, tell me, didn't you know that I had issued a decree forbidding this?

ANTIGONE

I knew. How could I not know? Everyone knew.

CREON

And yet you dared to break the law?

ANTIGONE

Yes. Because this order did not come from the gods above
nor those below and I didn't think that any edict issued
by you had the power to override the unwritten and
unfailing law of the gods. That law lives not only for
today or yesterday, but forever. I did not fear the judgement of a mere man so much as that of the immortal
gods. I knew I would die some day. Of course I knew –
even if you hadn't made your proclamation. And if I must
die before I have a chance to live, well, then, so be it.
Anyone who has been living as I have, buried alive in
sorrow, thinks death a blessing. For me death holds no
pain, but if I had left my brother unburied, for that I
would have suffered. It is a fool who calls what I have
done foolish.

CHORUS

Savage child of a savage father. Suffering has taught her
nothing.

CREON (addressing CHORUS and audience)

It's the stubborn spirit that's more prone to fall than
others; it's the toughest iron that snaps and shatters. I
have seen wild horses tamed by a small bridle. Arrogance
does not suit a young girl. She showed her insolence when
she broke the law, and that's not all. It was one crime to
do it, but to boast about it afterwards? If she gets away
with this, she is the man – not I. Even if she is my sister's

child, and closer in blood than any other member of our house, she and her sister will not escape punishment. Oh, yes, the other is equally guilty. Call her; a moment ago I saw her inside, ranting and out of her wits. The mind often betrays the criminal, even when he plots his evil in the dark.

(*Turning to* ANTIGONE.) But what I hate most is someone who's caught putting a good face on the crime!

ANTIGONE

Will my death satisfy you?

CREON

That's all I want.

ANTIGONE

So why postpone it? There's nothing you can say that will change the way I feel. Nor can anything I say change your feelings about me. But I don't care. There's no greater glory than this for me – the burial of my brother. Everyone here would cheer me, if fear didn't silence them. But the tyrant is lucky: he can do and say what he likes with impunity.

CREON

You are the only one who thinks so, Antigone.

ANTIGONE

Oh, no, they agree with me, Creon, but they have to be careful what they say to you.

CREON

Have you no shame?

ANTIGONE

There is no shame in what I have done for my brother.

CREON

Wasn't the one who died defending his country a brother too?

ANTIGONE

Yes, Eteocles was also my brother, by the same mother and the same father.

CREON

Then why do you dishonour one by giving honour to the other?

ANTIGONE

My dead brothers would not look at it that way.

CREON

Oh yes, Eteocles would if he got no more honour than a traitor.

ANTIGONE

Polyneices was not simply a traitor; he was Eteocles' brother.

CREON

One brother attacked his country; the other defended it.

ANTIGONE

The gods require that the same laws of burial be observed for both.

CREON

Traitors and heroes do not have the same rights.

ANTIGONE

Who knows who is traitor or hero in the land of the
dead?

CREON

An enemy will never be one of us, even if he is dead.

ANTIGONE

I was born to love, not to hate.

CREON

Then go love in hell. As long as I'm alive, no woman will
tell me what to do.

Enter ISMENE.

CHORUS

Look, Ismene is coming through the gates weeping for her
beloved sister and brothers. Her face is flushed and tears
are pouring down her cheeks.

CREON

I didn't realise you were a snake lurking in my house,
ready to poison me, and that I was raising two traitors. So
tell me, did you or did you not share in this burial?

ISMENE

Yes, I did. If she says so, then I share the blame.

ANTIGONE

Justice won't let you: you refused and I did it alone.

ISMENE

I'm prepared to suffer with you.

ANTIGONE

Those below know who did it; I need more than words.

ISMENE

Don't despise me, sister: I want to die with you and pay respect to the dead.

ANTIGONE

Don't try to die with me and don't take the blame for something you didn't do; it is enough that I die.

ISMENE

Without you what reason do I have for living?

ANTIGONE

Ask Creon. You supported him.

ISMENE

Why do you want hurt me, Antigone? Why?

ANTIGONE

I don't mean to hurt you. I'm just telling the truth.

ISMENE

I want to help you.

ANTIGONE

Then save yourself: I don't want you to die too.

ISMENE

Oh, pity me. Let me die with you.

ANTIGONE

No. You chose life, and I, death.

ISMENE

I only said what I believed.

ANTIGONE

Some will think you are right; others will think I am.

ISMENE

We're both guilty now.

ANTIGONE

No! You live; as for me, I dedicated my life to the dead a long time ago.

CREON

You're insane, the pair of you.

ISMENE

Suffering drives out good sense, Creon.

CREON

You lost your good sense when you chose to side with a criminal.

ISMENE

I can't live without my sister.

CREON

Don't speak of her; she is as good as gone.

ISMENE

Will you kill your son's future bride?

CREON

There are other furrows for him to plough.

ISMENE

He won't find another like her to love.

CREON

Thank god! If he married her he would have had a criminal in his bed.

ISMENE

O Haemon, you too are a victim of your father's cruelty!

CREON

You're exhausting my patience, Ismene.

ISMENE

Will you really steal Antigone from your son?

CREON

It will be death that stops that marriage. Not me.

ANTIGONE

So you've decided I'll die.

CREON

Yes. We've both decided, so let's stop wasting time. Take them inside! From now on they must realise that they are women and are not free to roam where they like. Guard them well. Death can make even the most reckless think of escape.

ANTIGONE *and* ISMENE *are led away.*

CHORUS

Happy are they whose life has no taste of sorrow.
Once their house falls from grace,
They are cursed, generation after generation,
Like the muddy sea swell
When a cruel Thracian wind stirs up black sand
From the ocean's floor.
The shores struck by this ill wind moan and shriek.

The sorrows of the living pile up
Over the sorrows of the dead:
There is no peace for any generation;

The gods strike them down,
And there is no escape.
In the house of Oedipus,
The light shining over the last roots
Is extinguished by the bloody burial owed the gods,
By thoughtless talk, and a hell-bent mind.

For the gods have the power and the glory!
Who can challenge them?
Sleep has no power over them,
Nor the ceaseless stream of days.
Ageless and timeless,
The gods dwell in the flashing splendour of Olympus.
Mankind is different.
His happiness, like his life, is fragile.
One law governs past, present, and future:
Happiness does not last.

The hope we all have in our hearts
Leads some to profit,
Others it lures into empty longing;
Only the pain of experience's fire can teach wisdom.
A wise man said
Bad seems good to the mind of him
Whom the gods would destroy.
He is happy for only a moment before disaster.
Happiness is the shortest candle of all:
Light for one minute, then darkness.

Enter HAEMON.

Here's Haemon, the last of your children; I think he's
heard the news about Antigone, and that his hopes for
marriage are now ruined.

CREON

I can see that for myself. Son, did you hear my decision
about your bride? Are you angry with me? Or are we still
friends?

HAEMON

Father, I am yours. You have the wisdom to direct me,
and I'll follow you. No marriage means more to me than
your wise guidance.

CREON

Right! That's a good son: he follows his father. People
pray to have obedient sons − allies for their fathers,
punishing enemies and honouring friends. But the man
who has useless children has sown tears for himself and
laughter for his enemies.

No, I say it clearly, son, never lose your mind over a
woman: if you have a bad wife, the bed soon grows cold
and she'll poison your life. Throw her out, like the trash
she is; let her find a husband in hell. Your Antigone is the
only person in the city who defied me and I caught her
in the act. I have no choice but to punish her as I would
any traitor. She can appeal to family ties all she wants,
but if I allow disobedience in the family, I can expect it
from the people too.

A good family man will always be a good citizen. We
cannot afford lawbreakers. We have to obey the man
whom the city appoints as leader in all his decisions large
or small, just, and if necessary, unjust. The man who
knows the virtue of obedience can be either a good ruler
or a good subject, and if he stands next to me in the
storm of battle, he'll be a strong, brave, and reliable

companion. There is nothing worse than anarchy. It
disrupts families and destroys cities. Obedience saves lives
and keeps the ship of state on the true course. We need to
preserve discipline and must never let ourselves be
defeated by a woman. If you must be beaten, be beaten
by a man; don't ever let yourself be called a woman's
plaything, my son.

CHORUS

You make a lot of sense.

HAEMON

Father, the most precious of all possessions the gods give
men is intelligence. I cannot say, nor would I ever want to
be in a position to say, that you are wrong. I know it is
not in your nature to care what people may be saying, or
doing, or with what they disagree. You terrify most people
and they are afraid to confront you. I, on the other hand,
can go about the city unrecognised, and I have heard
people weeping for this young woman, saying that the last
thing she deserves is to die for an act of great nobility.
Yes! She would not allow her brother who died in battle
to lie unburied, to be mauled by savage dogs and wild
birds. Surely she deserves to be honoured rather than
condemned? That is what they are whispering.

There is nothing that I want more, father, than your well-
being. What can please a son more than his father's
happiness and reputation – and a father in turn cannot
wish more for his son. Be open-minded, and don't think
that your opinion and no other is right. A man who
thinks he is the only one who makes sense, or talks well,
or has a mind, merely shows his own limitations. A wise

man can always learn – there's no shame in that – and learn not to be too set in his ways. In winter storms the trees that bend save themselves, but those that resist are destroyed root and branch. It's the same with a ship: in a strong wind, if you sheet in the sails too much, the boat will capsize. Get over your anger and be willing to change your mind. If you will forgive me preaching to you, father, I would say it's best to be born all-wise, but since this is rare, next best is to listen to good advice.

CHORUS

Sir, he has spoken well; why can't you learn from him? And you too Haemon, from your father: you both have a point.

CREON

So, am I, leader of the city, in my mature years, in full possession of all my powers, to be taught by an immature boy like you?

HAEMON

Only if I'm right; consider what I say, not my age.

CREON

Are you saying we should accept anarchy?

HAEMON

No!

CREON

But can't you see that that's what she is doing, breeding anarchy.

HAEMON

The people of our city don't think so.

CREON

Now it's the city that tells me how I should rule?

HAEMON

Father, you're behaving like a child. No city belongs to one man.

CREON

Doesn't the city's authority come from its ruler?

HAEMON

You're not ruling a desert, father, but a city full of people.

CREON (*to* CHORUS)

She's poisoned his mind against me.

HAEMON

No; I'm on your side.

CREON

Aren't you ashamed to stand there and question your father in front of others?

HAEMON

Not when I see him acting unfairly.

CREON

What is unfair about respecting and discharging the responsibilities of my office?

HAEMON

But you show no respect – you trample on the gods!

CREON

And you trample on filial piety! You are worse than a woman!

HAEMON

I'm not ashamed of what I've said, father.

CREON

You can't stop pleading her case, can you!

HAEMON

I am pleading for you too, for me, and for the gods below.

CREON

She will not live to marry you!

HAEMON

If she dies she'll take someone else with her.

CREON

So now you have the gall to threaten me!

HAEMON

There is no threat in telling you the truth.

CREON

You'll be sorry for this. You don't understand anything.

HAEMON

If you were not my father, I would say that you had lost your senses.

CREON

You're completely in her power! Stop wasting my time!

HAEMON

Won't you listen to a thing I'm saying?

CREON

I've had enough! By God, I'm not going to stand here
and let you insult me a moment longer! I'll teach you!
Drag out that viper, so she can die here on the spot, next
to her bridegroom.

HAEMON

I'll never let that happen. She won't die next to me. I'm
leaving. Do your worst father. You will never see me again.

Exit HAEMON.

CHORUS

Sir, he's left in a fury; a young mind stung with pain is
dangerous.

CREON

He can do what he wants; he can get drunk on his grand
ideas, but he will not save those two girls from death.

CHORUS

So you are going to kill them both! (*Pause.*)

CREON

No, you are right! Not the one who didn't touch the corpse.

CHORUS

How do you plan to kill Antigone?

CREON

I'll take her to some remote place and bury her alive in a
rocky hollow, giving her just enough food so the city will
escape pollution from her death. She can pray to the gods
of the underworld (they are the only ones she worships)
and ask them to spare her life; she may finally learn that
it is wasted effort to revere a dead traitor.

Exit CREON.

CHORUS

Passion always wins the fight;
Passion ravishes all.
You pass the night on the soft cheeks of a girl;
You wander over the sea and visit the
Haunts of those who live in the wild.
No immortal can escape you,
Nor that creature of a day – man.
All who are passion's slaves are mad.

You tear the just away from justice
Into violence;
It is you who have stirred up this fight between blood
    relatives.
Passion is always victorious; it flashes from the eyes
Of the beautiful bride as she is taken to bed.
The goddess Aphrodite has her throne next to the mighty
    laws.
When she plays her game with you,
She will win!

Enter ANTIGONE, *escorted by* GUARDS.

The sight of Antigone loosens the knot of loyalty.
I cannot hold back the fountains of tears
That spring forth when I see her
Going to her bridal chamber of eternal sleep.

ANTIGONE

Fellow citizens of this place that I call home,
Look on me as I go on my last walk,

To see the sun's rays for the last time,
And never again.
Hades of everlasting sleep
Brings me to the shores of Acheron.
Now I go to marry death,
But there will be no one to sing for me
At my wedding.

CHORUS

You have fair fame and praise
As you go to the cave of the dead!
Not wounded by wasting disease,
Nor suffering death from the sword,
But by your own free will,
Alone and alive,
You will descend to Hades.

ANTIGONE

I was told the story of Niobe
The saddest of all women.
She was near steep Sipylus,
And the rock embraced her;
Like ivy the stone clung to her;
Now the rain and snow constantly assail her
In her sorrow, or so men say;
And she bathes the ridges
With tears that do not cease.
Most like her am I,
Whom the gods send now to sleep.

CHORUS

But she is a goddess and born from gods,
And we are mortal and born from men.

Yet for the dead it is a great thing
To share in the fair fame of the gods,
Both in life and then in death.

ANTIGONE

So you're laughing at me.
Why do you insult me while I'm alive?
Can't you wait until I'm dead?
O city, O prosperous citizens,
O fountains of Dirce and forest of fair-charioted Thebes,
I call on you to witness how unwept by friends,
And under what cruel laws,
I go to my rocky prison, my strange tomb.
Oh, misery, I shall be housed
With neither the living nor the dead.

CHORUS

My child, you passed the limit of daring
And now you will be sacrificed on the high altar of justice.
Your crime adds to the crimes of the house of Oedipus.

ANTIGONE

You have touched a wound in me,
Painful memory of my father,
And of all the famous Labdacids,
That thrice-sung ode to sorrow.
Oh the horrors of sharing a mother's bed:
My father bedding the woman who bore him.
To such parents I owe my wretched birth;
Cursed and unmarried, I go to share their house.
Woe Polyneices for your fatal marriage:
When you died you slew me too!

CHORUS

Your reverence for your brother deserves respect,
But legitimate power must not be crossed.
It was your own choice,
Your passionate anger destroyed you!

ANTIGONE

Unwept, without friends, unsung,
Misery itself,
I travel the road before me.
All wretched, no longer may I
Look on the holy eye of the sun's light
And no friend weeps for my death.

Enter CREON.

CREON

If moaning could postpone death, no one would ever stop
crying! Take her away at once and block up the entrance
as I've ordered. Leave her there alone; it is her choice
whether she lives or dies. Our hands are clean: we leave
her in her grave with food and water. We are only
depriving her of the company of the living.

ANTIGONE

O tomb, my bridal chamber, home beneath the earth,
where I go to join my own. Many of them have already
been received into the house of death. I join the list, and
since I die unjustly before my time, my death is the worst
of all. I feed upon the hope I shall be welcomed by my
dear father and you my sweet mother, and by you my
dear brothers: with my own hands I washed you all and
prepared your bodies for burial; then I poured drink
offerings on your tombs. For tending your body,

Polyneices, see what I suffer. Wise people will say that
I did well to honour you. I would not have acted in this
way, in defiance of the state, if I had been the mother of
children, or if my husband had died. Why? If my husband
had died, I could have remarried, or if I'd lost a child,
I could have borne another, but since my mother and
father are both dead, no new brother of mine can be
born. That is why I honoured you my sweet brother, but
Creon calls it transgression and reckless crime. Now he
leads me alive into the hollowed out womb of the dead,
I, who know not the marriage bed, nor the bridal hymn,
who shall never raise a child, but alone, deprived of
friends, a wretched creature. What law of the gods did
I violate? Why am I wasting my time praying to the gods?
Whom can I call to stand by my side? I honoured what
should be honoured, and yet stand convicted of dishonour.
If the gods think that my punishment is deserved, then
I forgive my executioner. But if instead he is guilty, I curse
him and I demand that the gods make him suffer the
same pain he unjustly inflicts on me.

CHORUS
The same passionate wind still blows through her spirit.

CREON
Get her out of here NOW: if you're slow you'll be sorry!

ANTIGONE
O God, this command brings me closer to death.

CREON
Yes. There's no escape, Antigone.

ANTIGONE

O Theban city, land of my ancestors,
Gods of my forefathers,
They lead me away and there is no more time.
Look on me, rulers of Thebes,
The last of the royal line,
See what I suffer and who causes it
Because I honoured what should be honoured.

Exit ANTIGONE.

CHORUS

Imprisoned in a tomb-like chamber,
Danae also had to leave the light of heaven
For a bronze-bolted home.
She, too, was of an honourable line, my child,
Guardian of the golden flowing seed of Zeus.
But the force of fate is fierce;
Neither wealth, nor war, nor defending wall,
Nor black wave-battered ships offer escape.

The hasty-tempered son of Dryas,
King of the Edonians, was held prisoner.
Dionysus bound him in a rocky prison
As punishment for his stinging anger;
The brilliant flower of his frantic passion
Drooped and withered.
He learned what it was to taunt a god
With a mocking tongue.
He tried to stop the women
Filled with god and Bacchic fire
And harassed the music of their pipes.

By the shores of the Bosporus,
With its double sea-dark waters,
Is Thracian Salmydessus.
Ares, the city's neighbour,
Saw the accursed wound
The savage wife of Phineus
Dealt to their two sons:
She blinded them,
Wrenching the orbs of their eyes
From their sockets
With her bloody hands
And the sharp tips of her distaff.
This crime calls for vengeance.

The children wasted away weeping,
Sobbing a sad sorrow,
Offspring of a mother
Unblest in her marriage.
By birth she belonged
To the ancient house of Erechtheus,
But was raised in the caves of her father, Boreas;
Cuddled by his cold blasts,
She rode the steep hills,
Free with her companions;
She was born of the gods,
But the relentless fates
Also pressed hard upon her.

Enter TEIRESIAS.

Teiresias! Does he have something to tell us?

TEIRESIAS

Elders of Thebes, this boy and I have travelled this road
together, one seeing for both of us; the blind need a
guide.

CREON

What do you want, Teiresias, old man?

TEIRESIAS

I want nothing; just listen and obey.

CREON

I haven't disobeyed your commands in the past.

TEIRESIAS

And so you steered the ship of state well!

CREON

I will admit that I have benefited from your help.

TEIRESIAS

Good. Then know that you are once again on the razor's
edge.

CREON

What are you talking about? Your words frighten me.

TEIRESIAS

You will learn after you have heard what the signs have
revealed to me. I took my ancient seat of prophecy, where
birds of all kinds congregate, and I heard strange noises
coming from them, a meaningless screech of madness;
I knew they were ripping each other with bloody claws:
I could tell this from the whirring of their wings. Suddenly
I was afraid and tried to make a sacrifice on the lighted
altar, but the fire refused my offerings: they wouldn't

burn. A stinking slime from the thigh bones dripped down on the ashes and it smoked and sputtered, and gall from the livers spurted up into the air; the dripping thigh bones lay bare of their covering fat. It was useless to get a message out of the mess that my boy described to me: he is my guide as I am a guide for others. It is your decree, Creon, that has brought sickness on the city. Our altars and braziers are filled with the offal that birds and dogs deposit there: pieces of Polyneices, who fell in battle, that ill-fated offspring of Oedipus. The gods no longer receive either the prayers that we offer nor the flames from sacrificial thigh bones, and the birds no longer cry out clear messages for me, because they have eaten fat mixed with a dead man's blood.

Think about this, my son, there is not a man born who does not make mistakes. But if he is flexible and tries to correct his mistakes, he's both wise and fortunate. Egotistical stubbornness is mere stupidity. Stop kicking a dead man. What victory is there in dealing further blows to the dead? I want to help you, so I am giving you good counsel: it should be a pleasure to learn from an advisor if you stand to gain from his advice.

CREON

Old man, you have joined the others in attacking me, and your prophecies just add to my wounds. You soothsayers have made money out of me for years by bringing me terrible news. Count your gains, bring in your nuggets from Sardis and your gold from India. But you'll not bury that man, not even if the eagles of Zeus carry the pieces of his corpse up to high heaven! Pollution does not frighten me. I know that no mortal can pollute the gods.

And you, Teiresias, watch out! Even the cleverest fall and fail when they cloak their shameful message in glib words for the sake of gain.

TEIRESIAS
I have a piece of advice for you.

CREON (*interrupting impatiently*)
What? Still more advice?

TEIRESIAS
Sound judgement is the most precious of all possessions.

CREON
Yes, but I also know that talking nonsense causes greatest harm.

TEIRESIAS
That is the disease you suffer from!

CREON
I would tell you what I think, but I don't want to insult a prophet.

TEIRESIAS
You insult me when you dismiss my prophecies.

CREON
Prophets are all money-grubbers.

TEIRESIAS
And tyrants love bribes.

CREON
Don't you realise who it is you are talking to? I am your ruler!

TEIRESIAS

Of course I do; you are the ruler because of me: I am the one who helped you save the city.

CREON

You are a skilful prophet, but you also flirt with dishonesty.

TEIRESIAS

You are provoking me to say things which are better left unsaid.

CREON

Say your worst and make sure you collect your fee.

TEIRESIAS

I'm not speaking for gain – certainly not for yours!

CREON

Today you will learn that you can't sell your influence over me.

TEIRESIAS

And you will learn! Before the sun's chariot has run many courses, you will give up a child from your home, a corpse in payment for corpses. You buried one who should have remained alive on the earth. You put in a tomb a living being, while you kept unburied a corpse which belongs to the gods below. You should not have done this, and your violation has also polluted the gods above. Now you can never escape the avenging furies of hell, and they have set an ambush for you. See if I have been bribed to say this – you won't have long to wait to hear the weeping of men and women in your house. Since you provoked me, These are the arrows that I have shot directly into your heart, and I guarantee you will not escape the consequences.

Child, take me home, so he can rage against younger men, and learn to keep a quieter tongue and a mind more tractable than the one he has now.

Exit TEIRESIAS.

CHORUS
Sir, your man has made terrible prophecies. I know that in all my years, he has never lied to the city.

CREON
I know that. My mind is spinning. I think it is wrong for me to give in, but if I don't, I'm afraid I may be caught in a fatal web.

CHORUS
Think carefully.

CREON
Tell me what I should do and I'll do it.

CHORUS
Go and free the girl from her rocky chamber and build a tomb for the exposed corpse.

CREON
Is that your advice? So you're telling me to give in?

CHORUS
As quickly as possible, sir – swift-footed vengeance is on its way.

CREON

Oh God, it's so hard (*Pause.*) . . . but I'll do it. I can't
fight the inevitable.

CHORUS

Go then and do it yourself; don't leave it to others.

CREON

I'll go at once; call my attendants to help me. Since I see
what I did was wrong, I'll go free her myself. Oh, I'm
afraid...

Exit CREON.

CHORUS

God of many names,
The delight of Semele,
Offspring of Zeus the god of thunder,
O Bacchus,
You who watch over noble Italy,
And rule the hollow valleys of Eleusinian Demeter,
Which are open to all,
You who live in Thebes,
The mother city of the Bacchantes,
Next to the flowing stream of Ismenus,
Near where the wild dragon's seed was sown.

Burning pitch lights your way
Above the two-crested peak
When the Corycian nymphs
Roam in your honour near the Castalian spring.
The Nysian mountain's slopes of ivy
And the green shores covered with grapes
Attend your procession;

Immortal voices sing your praises,
When you walk the streets of Thebes.

You honour this city above all cities
Along with your mother blasted by lightning;
And now to your citizens stricken with disease,
Come, healer,
Over the slopes of Parnassus
Or across the moaning sea-narrows.

Hail lord of the dance of the fire-breathing stars,
Priest of night voices, son of Zeus,
Appear lord, with your Thyiads by your side,
Dancing all night their frenzied figures
In honour of their lord Iacchus.

Enter MESSENGER.

MESSENGER

You who live in Cadmus's city, home of Amphion, life is
so unpredictable that one must beware of praising or
blaming prematurely. Luck constantly changes: now a
person's happy, now he's miserable. No mortal can predict
the future. Creon was once to be envied, or at least so I
thought, since he saved our Cadmeian land from its
enemies, took it on as his responsibility, guided it in
single-handed rule, and he was blessed with princely sons.
Now all has turned to nothing, for when a man must give
up all his joys, I don't think he lives, but instead he's a
corpse that breathes. Rejoice in great wealth all you like
and live in a palace, but if there is no happiness in your
life then all is worthless smoke and shadow.

CHORUS

What bad news do you have for us?

MESSENGER

They are dead and the living are responsible for their deaths.

CHORUS

Who is dead? Who is the murderer?

MESSENGER

Haemon, whose name rightly means blood, is dead.

CHORUS

Who killed him?

MESSENGER

He killed himself, angry at the murder his father committed.

CHORUS

Teiresias: your word has come true.

MESSENGER

Yes, you are right, and now we have to deal with it.

Enter EURYDICE.

CHORUS

I see poor Eurydice, Creon's wife, coming from the house. I don't know whether by chance or because she has heard about her son.

EURYDICE

Citizens, as I was unlocking the gate before going out to pray, I overheard talk of some disaster; I fainted with fear and fell back into the arms of the servants. Tell me what it is; please, I am not unused to hearing bad news.

MESSENGER

I was there and I shall tell you, dear Madam, and I shall not leave out one word of the truth. Why should I try to soothe you with kind words which will later make me a liar? Truth is always best.

I went along with your husband to the edge of the field where the body of Polyneices was still lying, ripped apart by dogs. We prayed to gods and goddesses of the underworld, asking them to be merciful. We washed the body with ritual water, and pulled up bushes to make a pyre and burned what was left of him. Heaped high with his native earth, we built a tomb, and then went to the girl's bridal chamber of death with its bed of stone.

While we were still some way off, we heard a shrill cry from the unholy tomb, and we ran to tell our master Creon. As Creon drew nearer, he heard an indistinct cry of pain, and when closer, he moaned in bitter agony: 'Oh terrible, have I guessed right? Am I on the loneliest path I have ever walked? Is it my son's voice I hear? Come on, all of you, run closer and look inside, and tell me if this is the voice of Haemon, or is it a trick of the gods.' We looked as our despairing master told us, and we saw her at the back of the tomb hanging by her neck from a noose of knotted linen. Haemon was embracing her with his arms around her waist. He wept for the loss of his bride, and the acts of his father which destroyed his hope of marriage. When Creon saw him, he went up to him and let out a piercing cry of pain, 'What are you doing

here? What are you thinking? Are you mad? Come out
at once! I beg you; I'm pleading with you!' His son glared
at him with wild eyes and spat in his face. Wordlessly,
Haemon drew his long two-edged sword and lunged at his
father, who dodged away; then, furious with himself, the
poor lad straight-away fell upon his sword, driving its full
length right through his body. Still conscious he embraced
the girl again with his free arm, and as he breathed a kiss,
a sharp stream of blood jetted from his lips to stain her
white cheek and consummate their union in death. The
corpses lay there in their last embrace. The poor boy was
married, but by death.

Exit EURYDICE.

CHORUS
Our queen has left without a word. What does this mean?

MESSENGER
I hope now that she has heard of her son's death she will
not demand public mourning, but will keep it indoors, as
it should be, a household lamentation. She is not without
discretion.

CHORUS
I'm worried: I think that both deep silence and wild wailing
are dangerous.

MESSENGER
If we go inside, we'll soon find out. You're right, too
much silence also has its dangers.

Exit MESSENGER.

Enter CREON *with the body of his son.*

CHORUS

Here's the king with the bitter fruit of his folly. His
destruction was his own fault, not anyone else's.

CREON

Oh, grim mistakes of my mad mind,
Stone-stubborn and heavy with death,
You see your family, those who slew and those who died!
Oh, I curse the blind folly of my decisions!
Oh my child, so young in your young death,
Aiai, aiai!
You died and were taken from me
Because of my own wrong-headedness, not yours.

CHORUS

Too late it seems you see where justice lies.

CREON

I have learned a bitter lesson:
The gods have struck a heavy blow,
Drove me down a cruel path,
Trampling on my joy.
O sorrows of man born to sorrow.

Enter MESSENGER.

MESSENGER

My lord, you have a store of sorrows: one you carry here
in your arms, but soon you will see another in your
house.

CREON

What is there that can be worse than this?

MESSENGER

Your wife is dead, the dead boy's mother,
poor creature, still bleeding from her fresh wounds.

CREON

Shame,
Shame for the insatiable house of Hades!
Why do you destroy me?
You messenger of evil bringing me pain,
What is this you are telling me?
Aiai, why kill me again? I am already dead.
What is this message you bring me?
Aiai, aiai!
New death upon old,
The death of my wife
Seizing me in her cold embrace.

CHORUS

She's here for you to see.

EURYDICE*'s body is brought in.*

CREON

Oh, God, I see her. What more could there be? I held my
child in my arms, and now must I see her dead body
before me? Oh poor mother, poor child.

MESSENGER

She killed herself with a sword near the altar....she closed
her eyes and welcomed the darkness, weeping for
Haemon. Finally she cursed you as the murderer of her
child.

CREON

Aiai, aiai!
My heart is racing; all I see is darkness. Please, someone,
Strike me down with a sword!
Free me from my misery!

MESSENGER

Your dying wife called you responsible for destroying both
her and your son.

CREON

How did she kill herself?

MESSENGER

She stabbed herself to the heart, so that she could feel the
same sharp pain that her son felt.

CREON

Oimoi...No one else is to blame for this. I did it, I killed
you, Oh God, I did it, it is true. You, there, lead me
away, throw me away, get rid of me: I am nothing and
less than nothing.

CHORUS

You are right, if there is any right in wrong. The quickest
way to death is the best, if the path is filled with such
sorrow.

CREON

Oh yes, oh yes, come, welcome death – show me my last
day, the best day of all because it is my last. Oh yes, yes,
may I not live to see another day.

CHORUS

That is in the future, and the future is in others' hands.
We must attend to the tasks before us.

CREON

I have prayed for what I most desire.

CHORUS

No prayers; man cannot escape the suffering the gods
have in store for him.

CREON

Take me away, useless creature that I am, I, who killed
my son, and also my wife; (*Looking at* EURYDICE.) Oh,
this pain, I don't know which way to look, which way to
lean; I destroyed everything I touched and I have no
strength left.

CHORUS

If a person is to be happy,
He needs good sense.
Never show disrespect to the gods.
Loud words from those with high pretensions
Lead to heavy blows of punishment;
Good sense is hammered out on the anvil of age.

Glossary

ACRISIUS (A, as in apt, KRIS-eeus, Greek A-KREE-si-os) found the mother and child in the tower and set them in a chest afloat on the sea to die, but Zeus saved them. Later Perseus did indeed accidentally kill his grandfather Acrisius. Sophocles wrote about this in two lost plays, *Danae* and *Acrisius*.

AIAI (EYE-EYE) a sound of lamentation like *Oimoi* (OY MOY).

BACCHANTS (Bahk-KANTS) were worshippers of Dionysus, the god of the theatre and of wine. They were traditionally shown as wild creatures, possessed by the god and ranging the mountains. In this translation Bacchant refers to the male worshiper and Bacchante the female. Bacchus is another name for Dionysus.

BOSPHORUS (BOS-for-us) the body of water that joins Propontis (Sea of Marmara) to the Black Sea, and its name (*Bosporus*: 'cow crossing') refers to Io crossing it in the form of a cow, like Danae, a victim of Zeus' lust. Ares was a patron god of the war-loving Thracians. Salmydessus was a city on the west coast of the Black Sea.

CADMUS (CAD-mus, Greek Kagmos) The Thebans were said to have been born from the teeth of the dragon slain by Cadmus, the founder of Thebes.

CASTALIAN (Cas-TAL-eean) SPRING is also close to Delphi and its waters purified those coming to the temple of Apollo; it is also sacred to Dionysus.

CORYCIAN (Cor-I, as in lift,-sion) CAVE is on Parnassus above Delphi, where both Apollo and Dionysus are worshipped.

DANAE (DA-nigh-eh, Greek DAH-nah-ay) was the daughter of Acrisius, king of Argos, and was told that she would bear a child that would kill him. He locked her in a bronze tower, but Zeus found his way in, coming as a shower of gold. Danae gave birth to the Perseus.

DEMETER (DEE-me-ter) is goddess of the earth, mother of Persephone who was taken off by Hades. She has special rites at Eleusis which help a soul enter Hades.

DIONYSUS (Die-oh-NIGH-suss, Greek Dee-OH-nee-sos) God of the wine and theatre, son of Zeus and Semele. The worship of Dionysus was imported by the Greeks who settled most of southern Italy.

DIRCE (DEER-key, Greek DEER-KAY) Dirce is a river near Thebes named after the brutal wife of Lycus, King of Thebes, who persecuted Antiope. She was slain by the sons of Antiope avenging their mother.

ERECHTHEUS (Eh-RECK-thyôos) was a mythical king of Athens and one of his daughters, Orithyia, was swept away by Boreas. She had four children by him, and one was Cleopatra. NYSA (NIGH-sah) is a mountain in Euboea where Dionysus is said to have been raised by Nymphs. Euboea was known for its wine, the gift of Dionysus.

HADES (HAY-dees, Greek AH-DAYS) is both the name of the underworld and of its king. Acheron is one of the rivers of Hades. The dead must cross it, with Charon as their ferryman.

HEPHAESTUS (Heh-PHY-stus, Greek Heh-PHY-stos), Hera's son, is the god of fire, and carpenter of the gods, married to Aphrodite.

IACCHUS (Ee-AH-cuss) is another name for Bacchus/ Dionysus.

LABDACUS (Lab-DACK-us, Greek Lab-DA-cos) is Cadmus' grandson, Laius' father, Oedipus' grandfather and Antigone's great-grandfather. One legend tells us that he opposed Dionysus' worship and, like Pentheus, was torn apart by Bacchantes for this outrage.

LYCURGUS (Lie-KUR-gus, Greek Lee-KUR-gos) the son of Dryas, was king of the Edonians in Thrace. He opposed the introduction of Bacchic rites and so was punished. One account says he was torn apart like Pentheus and Labdacus, but there are other versions. He may have been blinded (*Iliad* 6. 130-43) or forced to kill his son, or, as here, simply imprisoned. Aeschylus wrote a trilogy and a satyr play about Lycurgus.

NIOBE (Nigh-OH-bee, Greek Nee-OH-Bay) is the daughter of Tantalus, king of Lydia in Asia Minor. She married Amphion, king of Thebes. They had seven daughters and seven sons. Niobe boasted that she was more blessed than Leto who had only two children (Apollo, the god of archery and the sun, and music, and Artemis the goddess of the hunt and childbirth). Leto asked her children to avenge this insult, and they killed Niobe's children. The gods changed her into a rock cliff (visible on Mount Sipylus in Asia Minor). She still weeps ceaselessly: streams constantly flow from this cliff.

OEDIPUS (EE-di-puss, Greek OY-dee-pouse) Father of Electra and Ismene, Polyneices and Eteocles, husband of Jocasta, son of Laius.

PHAEDRIADES (PHI-dree-AH-dees, Greek PHI-dree-AH-des) are two cliffs above Delphi, part of the Parnassus range.

PHINEUS (FIN-ee-us, Greek FEE-nyôos) king of Salmydessus, who married Cleopatra. They had two sons. Some accounts say that Phineus remarried, and the step-mother Eidaea or Eidothea (daughter of Dardanus, who built Troy) put out the children's eyes. Only her childhood experience of a cave explicitly relates her to Antigone's imprisonment. Cleopatra's father was Boreas, god of the North Wind.

POLYNEICES (Poly-NICE-seize, Greek Poly-NEE-kays) Brother of Antigone, Ismene, and Eteocles. Polyneices' name in Greek means 'many quarrels,' 'much strife.'

SEMELE (SEH-meh-lee, Greek Se-me-leh) Daughter of Cadmus, Tricked by Hera, Semele asked Zeus to appear to her in divine form; he showed himself in the form of a thunderbolt and she was killed. He put Dionysus into his thigh which acted as a womb until the child was born.

THYIADS (THIGH-yads, Greek THEE-yads) are Bacchantes.

ZEUS (ZYOOS) King of the gods and men, God of thunder and lightning.